Arts and Crafts
of the
Native Americans

Ting Morris
Illustrated by Emma Young

A⁺

Smart Apple Media

Published by Smart Apple Media
2140 Howard Drive West, North Mankato, MN 56003

Artwork by Emma Young
Designed by Helen James
Edited by Mary-Jane Wilkins
Picture research by Su Alexander

Photograph acknowledgements
Front cover: Gunter Marx Photography/Corbis
page 5 & 6 Richard A Cooke/Corbis; 7 Lake County Museum/Corbis;
8 Werner Forman/Corbis; 9t Nevada Wier/Corbis, b Pete Saloutos/Corbis;
10 Buddy Mays/Corbis; 12 Christie's Images/Corbis; 13 David Muench/
Corbis; 14, 15, 16 & 18 Werner Forman/Corbis; 19t Stapleton Collection/
Corbis, b Burstein Collection/Corbis; 20 & 21t Seattle Art Museum/Corbis,
21b Werner Forman/Corbis; 22 Gunter Marx Photography/Corbis; 24
Corbis; 25 & 26 Werner Forman/Corbis; 27t Richard A Cooke/Corbis,
b Christie's Images/Corbis; 28 Werner Forman/Corbis

Printed in Singapore

Library of Congress Cataloging-in-Publication Data

Morris, Ting.
Native Americans / by Ting Morris ; illustrated by Emma Young.
p. cm. — (Arts and crafts of the ancient world)
Includes bibliographical references and index.
ISBN-13: 978-1-58340-916-9
1. Indian craft—Juvenile literature. 2. Indians of North America—Material
culture—Juvenile literature. I. Young, E. (Emma), ill. II. Title

TT22.M69 2006
745.5089'97—dc22   2006003131

First Edition

9 8 7 6 5 4 3 2 1

Contents

The world of the Native Americans

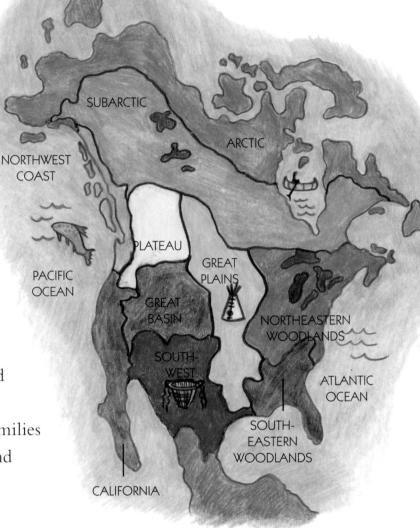

Many thousands of years ago, hunters in search of food crossed a narrow land bridge from Asia to North America. During prehistoric times, groups of families moved south. They crossed mountain ranges and rivers to reach vast forests, plains, and deserts.

Wherever they went, people fit in with their surroundings. This meant that the Native Americans developed skills and traditions that were suited to the places in which they lived. Families joined together and formed bands and larger groups, called tribes, in which everyone spoke the same language.

When European explorers arrived about 500 years ago and thought they had reached the Indies, they called the local people Indians. The newcomers wanted more land, and life changed for the Native Americans. But many of their traditions and customs,

This map of North America shows 10 different cultural regions. The Native Americans of each region led a similar way of life, but there were no real boundaries.

including their arts and crafts, live on through their descendants in the United States and Canada.

Mound builders

Some early Native Americans in the northeast woodland region built great mounds of earth. They dug and moved the earth without the help of animals or wheeled carts, yet they managed to create wonderful shapes, such as snakes, birds, and tortoises. We call the earliest moundbuilders Adena people, after the site in present-day Ohio where their remains were first found. The Adena produced most work from about 600 to 100 B.C. Some of their mounds were burial grounds, but the purpose of others remains a mystery.

In this photograph of Great Serpent Mound in Ohio, you can see the snake-shaped mound surrounded by a modern path.

People of the potlatch

Giving gifts has always been important in Native American culture. In the northwest region, the coastal people held a special ceremonial feast called a potlatch (from a Nootka word meaning "giving away"). At the feast, the host gave away huge amounts of property, including blankets, furs, and wooden chests. In this way, he showed how wealthy and important he was.

Farmers of the Southeast

The people of the southeastern region were farmers. Men cleared woodland for fields, and also hunted and fished. Women gathered wild plants and tended fields of corn and other crops. Powerful chiefdoms grew in the valley of the Mississippi River, and about 1,200 years ago, some farming villages became large towns.

One of the towns was at a place called Moundville, in present-day Alabama. Historians call this the Mississippian culture. The works of the artists and craftsmen were similar to those of the early people of Mexico, and the Mississippians may have been traders. Many of the later southeastern tribes, such as the Cherokee, are famous for their ceremonies and dances.

A dance mask. The maker probably added the features with his fingers, using charcoal or black walnut.

Cherokee dancers

Every year, the Cherokee and other tribes celebrated the ripening of the corn crop with dances and feasts. This was the Green Corn festival. The Cherokee were farmers and hunters who settled in the southern region of the Appalachian Mountains. For their Eagle Dance, the Cherokee collected eagle feathers and used them to make wands that they waved as they danced. They used their Booger Dance to defend themselves against outsiders, and this became even more important after the arrival of Europeans. Dancers wore masks that were made to look like the threatening strangers.

Seminole dress

The Seminoles are descendants of the Creek tribe. They moved from the southern woodlands to Florida in the early 18th century to avoid war with European settlers. Like other tribes of the region, the Seminoles made textiles from grasses and barks. Their favorite was the bark of the mulberry tree, which made a fine, light cloth. They colored the textiles with vegetable dyes or powdered minerals. Dressmakers often stitched strips of colored cloth onto dresses or sewed strips together in a technique called patchwork.

These Seminole children were photographed in Florida in the 1920s. They are wearing traditional dress.

Villagers of the Southwest

Around A.D. 800, the Anasazi people of the Southwest, who had settled in the region centuries earlier, began building villages. Their descendants were later called Pueblo (or village) people by Spanish explorers. They include the Hopi tribe of modern Arizona and the Zuni of New Mexico.

A Mimbres black-on-white bowl. It was used as a burial offering and had a hole punched through it so that the bowl was "dead" and its spirit released.

Another related group was the Mimbres people, who were great potters. Around A.D. 900, they began making black-on-white pots. They did this by rolling soaked clay into long coils. These were laid one on top of another and then pinched, scraped, and smoothed so that the joints could not be seen. The Mimbres painted on designs with a brush made of yucca leaves shredded at one end.

Turquoise jewelry

Blue-green turquoise was the favorite stone of the Pueblo people. They found it in the Cerrillos Hills of New Mexico, where their ancient mines can still be seen. They smoothed and shaped pieces of turquoise into beads by rolling them on other stones, such as sandstone. Many villages had workshops, where craftsmen made the beads into jewelry.

Weaving traditions

The Navajo, who arrived in the region hundreds of years ago, learned weaving techniques from the Pueblo people. Men picked and spun cotton, and then women dyed it. In earlier times, the men wove the thread on wooden looms. After the Spanish brought sheep to the country, their wool was used to make blankets and rugs, and women took over the looms. They taught their daughters, who often began weaving at the age of four or five. Modern Native Americans have kept up many of these traditions.

This girl wears traditional turquoise jewelry to a modern Navajo parade in Arizona.

This Navajo woman is weaving on a traditional fixed loom. She weaves the geometric design from the bottom up. The loom hangs from a crossbar supported by two upright posts.

Make a kachina doll

The Hopi and other tribes held ceremonies in honor of a group of spirits called kachinas. They believed that the spirits came from their home in the mountains every spring with messages for the people. They also sometimes brought rain. Adults gave their children kachina dolls to teach them about the spirits and to encourage them to behave well.

Make your own kachina doll

You will need: air-drying clay • a modeling tool • a sponge (for moistening) • acrylic paints • paint brushes • Popsicle sticks • bits of fabric (felt, fur, leather, etc.) • string • strong glue

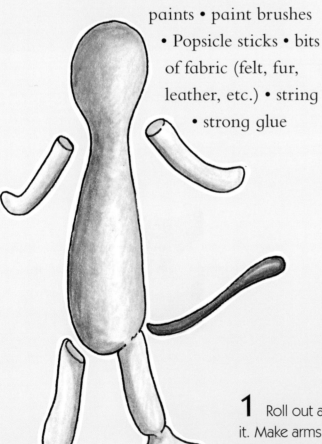

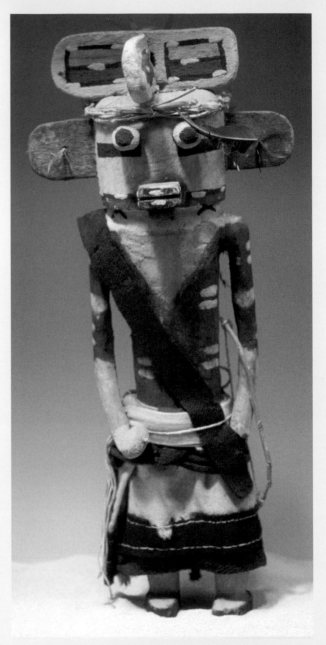

Early kachina dolls were made of cottonwood root. Later dolls, such as this one, were made of wood. Every kachina is different from other kachinas in some way.

1 Roll out a fat clay sausage and shape a body and head from it. Make arms with thin sausages, bending the ends to form hands. Mold legs and feet from smaller lumps of clay. Stick the limbs to the body by moistening the joints and smoothing them together.

2 Press small clay balls and strips into the head for the doll's eyes, nose, and mouth. Make the ears with Popsicle stick ends and push them into the clay. Make the spirit's crest with short sticks, or mold a clay crest on top.

3 When the doll is dry, paint it. Copy the colors of the Hopi kachina spirit. Leave the doll to dry, and then dress it, using pieces of leather, cloth, and fur. Make the hair with string. Stick everything on to the doll with strong glue.

A kachina doll was a Hopi child's first toy. Why not give this one to a small child?

Land of plenty

The region that is the state of California today had plentiful food for those who settled there. There were more than 60 tribes scattered in the area between the Pacific Ocean and the Sierra Nevada Mountains. Most lived in small villages, gathering acorns, berries, and seaweed; catching fish and shellfish; and hunting deer, elk, and sea lions.

This Pomo basket is decorated with tiny feathers and shells.

In the south of the region, tribes specialized in making tools and bowls from stone. The Gabrielino tribes quarried soapstone on the islands off the coast, and on the mainland, the Chumash people carved the soft stone into useful objects and ornaments.

Brilliant basketry

Pomo tribes lived in the north of the region. Each tribe had between 100 and 2,000 people, led by a headman or headwoman. Pomo women were expert basketmakers. Their materials were willow shoots, roots, and bark, and they used bulrushes to coil and twine their baskets.

Coiled baskets were made by winding and binding coils of fibers up from the base. Twining was a method of weaving strands over a framework of spokes. Pomo women made patterns with colored strands but never wound them

completely around the basket. There was a superstition that a complete pattern might make the basketmaker go blind.

Rock paintings

The Chumash and other Californian tribes painted pictographs, or picture symbols, on rocks and cave walls. No one is sure what the ancient symbols meant, but they were probably painted by shamans, or medicine men. Tribes may have used the caves as shrines or sacred places.

Most of the colors the painters used came from minerals. Red was from iron ore or ocher, white came from gypsum, and black from charcoal. These were ground into a powder and then mixed with water, animal fat, or plant sap. Painters applied the liquid colors with their fingers or with simple brushes made from animal hairs.

A Chumash painting inside a cave in the Californian desert.

On the Great Plains

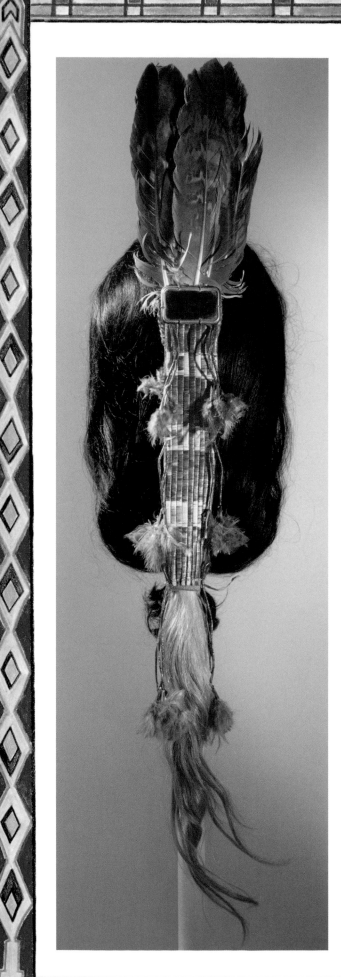

The Great Plains stretch from the Rocky Mountains in the west to the Mississippi River, and from the Canadian province of Alberta in the north all the way down to Texas. This vast region was once covered with grasslands. It was ideal territory for the hunting tribes who followed huge herds of buffalo across the plains.

Other tribes settled in farming villages, and every summer, they too moved out to the grasslands to hunt. Plains people lived off the buffalo, using its hide for clothing and shelter. They used the animal's bones as craft tools and scrapers, and rawhide became a canvas for storytelling pictures and designs.

Quillwork

Porcupines gave Plains tribes one of their best decorative materials—quills. Women pulled the thousands of quills out of a dead animal's body. They softened them in water, flattened them by pulling them through their fingernails or teeth, and dyed them with colors from blueberries

This Sioux hair ornament is made of red and white quills and feathers.

A young Cheyenne may have used this model tepee as a toy. It was painted with buffalo horns and tracks to give it the animal's power.

and other plants. Then they sewed or wove the quills onto hide. The patterns were in straight lines, because the quills were stiff and did not bend easily. Rectangles, crosses, and checks were most common. The women's quillwork was more than just decoration. They saw it as a way of praying for the safety of the man who wore the design.

Portable homes

Nomadic Plains tribes lived in buffalo-skin tents, called tepees, which they could put up and take down quickly. The tepee (a Sioux word meaning "dwelling") was made of skins stretched over a frame of wooden poles. Some tribes, such as the Blackfoot and the Sioux, painted designs on their tepees. They used brushes of willow, chewed cottonwood, or buffalo bone. In all of their art, men generally drew real people and animals, and women painted geometric patterns.

Make a feather headdress

Many Plains tribes were skillful featherworkers. For special headdresses, they attached the feathers of wild turkeys, hawks, herons, or eagles to a cap made of animal hide. On war bonnets, the number and type of feathers showed how successful the wearer had been in battle.

This war bonnet is made of eagle tail feathers. It belonged to an Arapaho chief.

Make your own headdress

You will need: lightweight cardboard 35 inches by 1 inch (90 x 3 cm) • a brown felt strip 30 inches by 2 inches (80 x 5 cm)• red and blue felt pieces for decoration • stiff white paper for feathers • thick red and black felt pens • 20 toothpicks • thin paper streamers • strong glue • tape • 6 colored ribbons 10 to 12 inches (25–30 cm) long

1 Ask a friend to help you make the cap. Put one cardboard strip around the head and tape the ends of the ring together. Attach another strip to the center back of the ring. Bring the strip over the top of the head to the front and tape it up.

2 Cut the brown felt into one 12-inch (30 cm) and two 9-inch (25 cm) strips. Make 20 feathers with stiff white cardboard, each 7 inches (18 cm) long and about 1.5 inches (4 cm) at its widest point. Color and cut the feathers. Tape the feathers on to toothpicks, leaving 1.5 inches (4 cm) at the bottom of each stick.

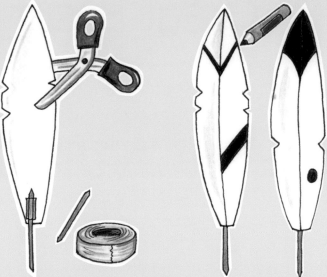

3 Attach six feathers to the longest of the three strips, leaving 1.5 inches (4 cm) at each end. Poke the toothpick in and out through the felt. This is the front of the headband. Attach seven feathers to each of the sidebands in the same way, leaving 1.5 inches (4 cm) at the top.

If you find any real feathers, you can add them to your headdress.

4 Glue the front strip to the cardboard front. Then glue the side strips in place, so that they hang down by your ears. Stick thin paper streamers to the ends of the feathers. Decorate the strips with felt shapes to cover up the toothpicks. Cut 2 blue felt circles about 2 inches (5 cm) in diameter and glue red and white ribbon behind each. Stick the ribbon discs onto the headband, as shown here.

17

Great Basin and plateau

The Great Basin region is a large area of desert that lies between the mountains of the Sierra Nevada and the Rockies. The high plateau is a smaller region to the north of the basin, with plenty of food. People of both regions were hunters, and they often crossed the Rocky Mountains to hunt buffalo on the plains.

Basketwork was an important craft to tribes such as the Nez Percé and Wasco. They coated their baskets with pine gum to make them waterproof, and they even used some as cooking pots. Hide painting was another popular craft, using buffalo or elk skins. Both men and women wore them as robes.

Cradleboards

Mothers carried small babies on a cradleboard. The board was generally made of wood, and the baby was attached to this in a sleeping bag made of soft leather and lined with fur or moss. The baby was comfortable and safe, and the mother had her hands free to work.

This buffalo hide robe was painted by a Shoshoni artist. The design at the top is made from quills.

A cradleboard photographed in 1910. The baby belonged to the Nez Percé ("pierced nose" in French) people, who were given their name by European explorers. They call themselves Nimi'ipuu, or "real people."

She carried the baby on her back and could lean the cradleboard against a tree when she rested. The boards and straps were decorated with beadwork or embroidery, and they often had special designs to bring good luck to the child.

Fun and games

Many tribes played the same or similar games throughout the region and all over the continent. Some were board games

played on decorated wooden trays or flat baskets. Players threw nut halves, acorn cups, or carved sticks onto the board. The winner was the person with the most counters the right way up, or the person who guessed the right number. In another game, one player laid sticks under a blanket, and the others had to guess which order the sticks were in.

The Klamath tribe played this four-stick game. The two pairs of sticks were placed or thrown into the bowl for guessing games.

Along the northwest coast

The homelands of the people of the northwest coast stretched
along the Pacific Ocean from southern Alaska to Oregon.
They built sea-going canoes to fish and catch whales.
The wood for their canoes and plank houses came from
large forests of redwood, fir, pine, and cedar.

The Chilkat tribe of the
Tlingit people wove
blankets like this, which
they wore as dancing
robes. Men made the
looms and designed
the patterns, and
women prepared the
mountain goat wool
and wove the blankets.

The men of the coastal villages were
great carvers of wood, bone, and ivory.
The women wove wonderful blankets,
mats, and baskets. Their arts and crafts
are often based on the legends they told
and show the importance of individuals
and families within each tribe.
Ceremonial feasts and dances formed
an important tradition (see page 5),
which inspired craftsmen and artists.

Catching souls

Coastal people believed in a world of
spirit beings. They also thought that a
shaman, or medicine man, could help
them reach the spirit world. The shaman
carved wooden masks and rattles used
in special ceremonies. This helped him
or her to cure illness or bring the right
weather for hunting and fishing. They
also carved objects called soul-catchers

This ivory soul-catcher is inlaid with shell. When a soul was caught by one of the two sea lions' mouths, it was plugged with a stopper to keep the soul in.

from walrus tusks. A shaman would use a soul-catcher to capture the soul of a sick person, which had left the invalid's body. When the soul was returned, the person got better.

Haida carving

Like many other groups of northwestern tribes, the Haida were great carvers. They made decorative prows for their large dugout canoes, totem poles for their houses (see page 22), and rattles and figurines for their shamans.

The Haida also made large chests from cedar wood, which they carved and painted with the owners' family crest. The chests were so well made that they were used to store fish oil. Craftsmen also carved mountain goat horns into ladles and spoons.

This ceremonial hat includes the carved wooden head of a wolf or bear. It was worn at potlatch feasts, and the eight rings show that the wearer had held eight successful potlatches.

Make a totem pole

The people of the northwest coast were famous for their tall wooden sculptures called totem poles. Free-standing poles were used as memorials or gravemarkers for chiefs. House poles were built into the front of wooden plank houses, and their size and painted carvings showed wealth and ownership of land and property. Well-known craftsmen carved symbols and animals that were important to the family. The owner's personal crest was usually placed on top of the pole.

The figure on top of this pole is a thunderbird. Only the most powerful chiefs could use the thunderbird crest. People believed that lightning flashed from the bird's eyes and that thunder rolled from its wings.

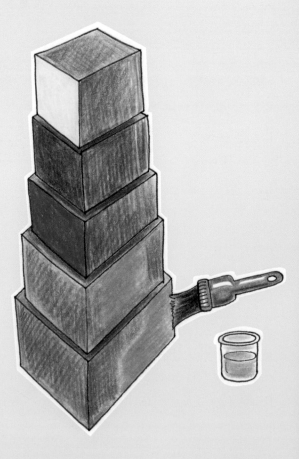

Make your own totem pole

You will need: 5 large cardboard boxes
• thin cardboard • colored paper • glue
• yellow, white, brown, red, and blue ready-mixed paints or powder paints • poster paints
• paintbrushes • masking tape

1 Seal the boxes with masking tape and stack them with the biggest box at the bottom. Paint the sides and backs of the boxes different colors. Give the front a thick, light brown undercoat as a base for the faces and markings.

2 Turn the bottom two boxes into a bear. Paint the bear's body on one box and its head with big teeth and a long tongue on another. When stacked, they should form a complete bear.

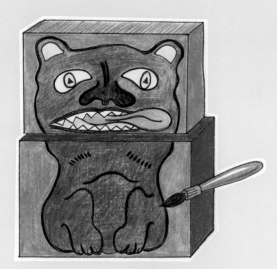

3 Curl a cardboard shape around the next box to look like a carving. Cut the cardboard so that it is big enough to fit around the front and the sides. Fold it in half and copy the outline (a). Cut along the line, open the folded paper and paint the face with Native American markings (b). Glue it to the sides of the box (c).

3a

3b

3c

4 Turn the top two boxes into the thunderbird. Cut two big cardboard wings and decorate them with feather-shaped pieces of colored paper. Glue the wings on the box.

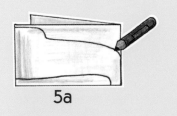

5a

5b

5 Copy the bird's beak onto a sheet of folded cardboard (a). Cut it out, paint it, and glue it to the front. Cut a crest from paper (b) and stick it on top of the thunderbird's head (c).

5c

Stack the boxes and set up the pole outside. Stop it from toppling by sticking the boxes together with a thick layer of glue.

The frozen North

The most famous people of the frozen Arctic region of present-day northern Canada are the Inuit. Their culture started around the coasts of the Bering Sea and the Arctic Ocean about 1,000 years ago. It has continued to this day, and in 1999, the Inuit were granted a Canadian territory, called Nunavut, as their homeland.

This Inuit woman was photographed in 1928. She wore beaded jewelry on her nose, ears, and lower lip. These ornaments were a sign of adulthood.

Farther south, in the subarctic region, various tribes moved through the dense forests, hunting caribou and moose. Craftsmen used the hair of these animals, as well as quills from porcupine spines and goose feathers, for embroidery. They made skillful use of beads made of shell, bone, copper, and seeds. After the Europeans arrived, they also traded glass beads.

Birchbark crafts

Algonquian tribes of the subarctic forests used the papery bark of birch trees to make all sorts of things. They peeled the bark from the trees with knives and used large sheets to make canoes, wigwams, cooking pots, and containers. The bark was also decorated, either by scraping away different colored

This Inuit finger mask has caribou hair around the small image of a face. The hair swayed as the wearer danced.

layers or by painting. The women of some tribes had a tradition of birchbark biting. They made patterns on the bark by biting it and marking it with their teeth.

Finger masks

Inuit women made small, wooden masks attached to single or double rings that they wore on their fingers. The masks usually had a human or animal face, often surrounded by fur, feathers, or caribou hair. Women dancers wore the masks, which made the dramatic movement of their hands more important than their feet. Inuit women made many other dolls and models, which they used to show their daughters how to carve and sew.

Woodland people

The northeastern woodlands region stretched from the Atlantic coast to the Mississippi River and included the area around the Great Lakes. There were two main groups of Native American tribes here. Some, such as the Shawnee, spoke an Algonquian language, while the Mohawk and the Huron spoke Iroquois.

Many of the Iroquois tribes were farmers. Some of the tribes specialized in making baskets from splints—strips of wood from the black ash tree. They also used birchbark. Another speciality was wampum, made from strings of white and purple beads, which was presented as a gift on ceremonial occasions. The Algonquian Fox tribe was famous for weaving with beads.

Early traders

The people of the early Hopewell culture, which flourished from about 100 B.C. to A.D. 500, were traders. Archaeologists have discovered a great deal about them from objects that were buried in their tombs south of the Great Lakes. The Hopewell people were farmers and traded shells and volcanic glass from farther south, and silver from north of the lakes.

On this Fox necklace, 40 grizzly bear claws are separated by pairs of beads. This necklace was a prized possession and could only be worn by someone who had shown great bravery.

This bird's claw was found in a Hopewell tomb. It was carved from mica, a kind of rock from the southeastern region.

They used these materials to make beautiful grave goods.

Moccasins

The word moccasin comes from the Algonquian *maskisina*, which described the soft hide shoes made and worn by people in the northeastern region. Native Americans made similar footwear across the continent. Most woodland designs were made of buckskin and beaded, quilled, or embroidered. They were essential equipment, and craftsmen made them all the time, as each pair might only last a few weeks.

A pair of beaded moccasins made by the Micmac, who lived near the Atlantic coast.

Make a false-face mask

Iroquois people of the woodlands thought that members of a group called the False Face Society had special healing powers. Society members wore wooden masks to make them look like ghostly figures they had seen in dreams. They were then able to cure people of illness.

An Iroquois false-face mask. It was carved from a living tree and worn at special ceremonies.

Make your own mask

You will need: newspaper • glue • a cardboard box or lid with strong corners • white ready-mixed paint • red, black, and white poster paints • a pencil • a bucket • elastic • paintbrushes • brown wool for hair • a craft knife

1 First, prepare the paper pulp. Tear newspaper into 1-inch (2.5 cm) squares. Fill a bucket with warm water, put the paper in, and leave it to soak. When it's soft, mash it and squeeze out the water. Pour in some glue and mash it into the pulp with your fingers until the mixture is like sticky dough. Keep it dry so that it holds its shape and you can model it.

2 Measure the length of your head and the width from ear to ear. Use these measurements to draw a mask on one corner of the box. Ask an adult to help you cut out the mask shape with a craft knife.

3 Hold the mask in front of your face and mark where your eyes, nose, and mouth come. Measure the points and mark them on the mask. Cut out small holes for the eyes, a breathing hole, and a mouth opening.

4 Cover the face with a layer of pulp and build up the features on your mask. According to the dream visions of the carvers, the mask has hollow eyes, a large, bent nose, a creased forehead, and grinning lips. Smooth the pulp with your hands. Then leave it to dry. This might take a few days.

5 When the mask is dry, paint it with white ready-mixed paint. Wait for this to dry, then paint it red like the mask shown here. Glue on long wool hair. Thread elastic through the sides and tie it in place.

The False Face Society believed that the colors represented the journey of the first False Face, who followed the sun. His face went from red in the morning to black in the evening.

29

Glossary

archaeologist A person who studies the ancient past by digging up and looking at remains.

buckskin The skin of a male deer used as leather.

buffalo A large, wild ox, also called a North American bison.

caribou A North American reindeer (from a Micmac word meaning "snow-shoveler").

ceremonial Having to do with ceremonies, especially important religious or public events.

charcoal A black form of carbon made by heating wood.

continent One of Earth's seven huge landmasses.

cottonwood A kind of poplar tree with seeds covered in cotton-like hairs.

cradleboard A wooden board with a pouch to hold and support a baby.

crest A symbol, usually an animal or a bird, that represents a family.

descendant A person related to someone who lived in the past.

elk A large kind of deer.

figurine A small figure or statuette.

geometric Having straight lines and regular shapes.

gypsum A soft, white mineral.

hide The treated skin of an animal.

kachina An ancestral spirit that Hopi and other Pueblo tribes believed lived in the mountains.

moccasin A soft hide shoe (from an Algonquian word for "shoe").

ocher An earthy, rusty substance that can be used to make a red color.

pictograph A picture symbol representing a word or an idea.

plaque A flat piece of wood, metal, or stone that is decorated or inscribed.

plateau A flat area of high land.

potlatch A ceremonial feast at which the host gave generous gifts (from a Nootka word meaning "giving away").

prehistoric In the time before people made written records.

prow The projecting front part of a boat.

quill The spine of a porcupine or the shaft of a bird's feather.

quillwork Crafts decorated with quills.

rawhide Untreated leather or skin, especially buffalo hide.

shaman A person who can contact the world of spirits and tell the future or heal people; sometimes called a medicine man.

shrine A sacred place of worship.

subarctic Relating to a region just south of the frozen Arctic.

superstition A belief in the magical effect of an action or event.

tepee (or tipi) A cone-shaped skin tent on a framework of wooden poles.

tradition Customs, beliefs, and ways of doing things that are passed down from generation to generation.

tribe A large group of families with the same beliefs, customs, and language.

wampum Strings of beads making up a belt or decoration (from an Algonquian word meaning "white string").

war bonnet A ceremonial headdress worn by some Native American warriors.

wigwam A dome-shaped hut or tent made of skins, matting or bark (from an Algonquian word meaning "house").

Index